A Guide to
AMERICAN STATES

Nevada

THE SILVER STATE

MEDIA ENHANCED BOOKS

AV²
BY WEIGL

ADDED VALUE • AUDIO VISUAL

www.av2books.com

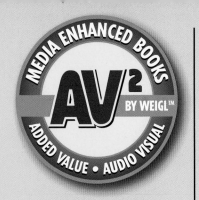

AV² provides enriched content that supplements and complements this book. Weigl's AV² books strive to create inspired learning and engage young minds in a total learning experience.

Your AV² Media Enhanced books come alive with...

Audio
Listen to sections of the book read aloud.

Key Words
Study vocabulary, and complete a matching word activity.

Go to **www.av2books.com**, and enter this book's unique code.

Video
Watch informative video clips.

Quizzes
Test your knowledge.

BOOK CODE

K 3 3 6 2 4 8

Embedded Weblinks
Gain additional information for research.

Slide Show
View images and captions, and prepare a presentation.

AV² by Weigl brings you media enhanced books that support active learning.

Try This!
Complete activities and hands-on experiments.

... and much, much more!

Published by AV² by Weigl
350 5th Avenue, 59th Floor
New York, NY 10118
Website: www.av2books.com   www.weigl.com

Library of Congress Cataloging-in-Publication Data

McLuskey, Krista, 1974-
 Nevada / Krista McLuskey.
    p. cm. -- (A guide to American states)
 Includes index.
 ISBN 978-1-61690-800-3 (hardcover : alk. paper) -- ISBN 978-1-61690-476-0 (online)
 1. Nevada--Juvenile literature. I. Title.
 F841.3.M383 2011
 979.3--dc23
                            2011018520

Printed in the United States of America in North Mankato, Minnesota

052011
WEP180511

Project Coordinator Jordan McGill
Art Director Terry Paulhus

Photo Credits
Every reasonable effort has been made to trace ownership and to obtain permission to reprint copyright material. The publishers would be pleased to have any errors or omissions brought to their attention so that they may be corrected in subsequent printings.

Weigl acknowledges Getty Images as its primary image supplier for this title.

Contents

Las Vegas is Nevada's most popular tourist destination.

Introduction

F or many people the state of Nevada centers on the glittering
city of Las Vegas. This year-round desert resort is famous for
wedding chapels in which Elvis **impersonators** conduct the
ceremonies. It is also known for its gambling **casinos** and luxurious
hotels, including one that is a glass **replica** of one of the Great
Pyramids of Egypt. Visitors to Las Vegas can see concerts, magic
shows, and comedians any day of the week. But there is more to
Nevada than the glitz and glamour of Las Vegas. The state's mild
winters draw people from all over the country. Beyond the blinking
neon lights is a diverse land of **barren** desert, snowcapped mountains,
and thousands of years of history.

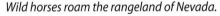
Wild horses roam the rangeland of Nevada.

Fly Geyser, located just north of Gerlach, was accidentally created by the drilling of a well in 1916.

Nevada's climate and land have historically been tough on residents. The desert was too dry to live on or to farm. The mountains were cold, and travel through them was difficult. Nevadans have found special ways to cope with the difficult climate. Cities have been built on the sand. Water has been transported to **irrigate** crops in the desert. The mountains have become sites for resorts that draw people from across the world.

Nevada's official nickname, the Silver State, recalls its early mining history. Another nickname, the Sagebrush State, comes from Nevada's abundant growth of the shrubby gray-green plant called sagebrush. Nevada is also sometimes called the Battle Born State because it was admitted to the Union in 1864, during the Civil War.

Where Is Nevada?

Nevada lies on rugged highland between the Sierra Nevada and Rocky Mountain ranges in the western United States. At one time Nevada was almost impossible to reach. Many people died trying to cross the mountains that make up its southwestern border. Today interstate highways and airports bring millions of tourists into the state with ease. Interstate 80 cuts through the northern part of the state and passes through Reno, the main transportation center for northwestern Nevada and northeastern California. In the south, Interstate 15 takes travelers to Las Vegas. Three major railroads cross the state.

Nevada's largest airport is McCarran Airport in Las Vegas.

Mineral production has long been a major industry in Nevada, and the state's early history was largely the story of its mining cycles. The region's population was sparse until the discovery of the silver deposits called the Comstock Lode in 1859. Virginia City, which is still a popular tourist attraction, grew almost overnight and was called "The Richest Place on Earth." The opening of the Comstock Lode and other deposits began a 20-year boom.

From about 1880 to 1900 there was little mining, and the population of Nevada declined. Another boom began after 1900 with silver and gold strikes at Tonopah and Goldfield and the development of copper mining at Ely. Another decrease in mining occurred in the period between the two world wars. World War II brought on a third boom in mineral production in the 1940s. After the war the economy thrived on the state's year-round resorts.

I DIDN'T KNOW THAT!

Nevada is divided into 16 counties. The capital, Carson City, is an independent city that is not part of any county.

Half of the nation's wild horses and wild **burros** live in Nevada.

Nevada is the seventh-largest state in the nation in land area.

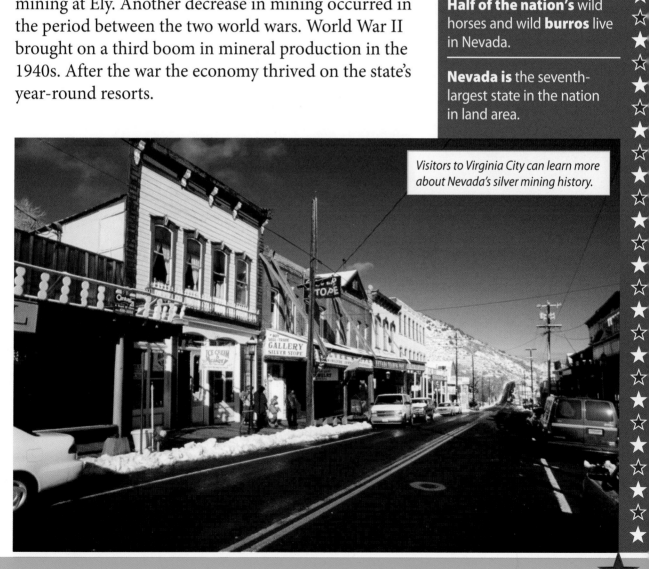

Visitors to Virginia City can learn more about Nevada's silver mining history.

Mapping Nevada

N evada borders California on the west and southwest, Oregon and Idaho on the north, Utah on the east, and Arizona on the southeast. It is the seventh largest state by size and located almost entirely in the Great Basin region of the United States. The majority of Nevada's population lives in the Las Vegas metropolitan area.

Sites and Symbols

STATE SEAL
Nevada

STATE BIRD
Mountain bluebird

STATE FLOWER
Sagebrush

STATE FLAG
Nevada

STATE ANIMAL
Desert Bighorn Sheep

STATE TREE
Bristlecone Pine

Nickname The Silver State

Motto All for Our Country

Song "Home Means Nevada" by Bertha Raffetto

Entered the Union October 31, 1864, as the 36th state

Capital Carson City

Population (2010 Census) 2,700,551 Ranked 35th state

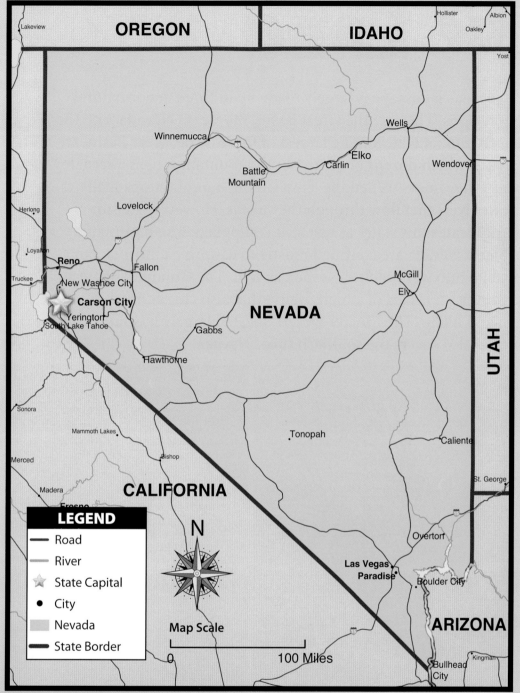

OREGON

IDAHO

Lakeview

Hollister

Albion

Oakley

Yost

Winnemucca

80

Wells

Elko

Carlin

Wendover

Battle
Mountain

McGill
Ely

Herlong

Lovelock

80

Loyalton

Reno

Fallon

NEVADA

Truckee

New Washoe City

Carson City

UTAH

Yerington

South Lake Tahoe

Gabbs

Hawthorne

Sonora

Mammoth Lakes

Tonopah

Caliente

Merced

Bishop

St. George

Madera

CALIFORNIA

N

Fresno

Overton

LEGEND

— Road
— River
⭐ State Capital
• City
▭ Nevada
— State Border

Map Scale

0   100 Miles

Las Vegas
Paradise

Boulder City

ARIZONA

Kingman

Bullhead
City

STATE CAPITAL

Carson City, with a population of more than 55,000, became Nevada's state capital in 1864. It Is the only capital Nevada has ever had.

United States

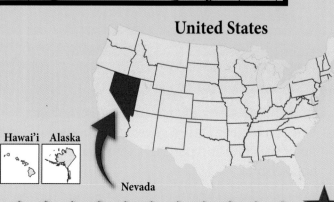

Hawai'i   Alaska

Nevada

The Land

Nevada's landscape is largely made up of three major natural regions. They are the Great Basin, the Sierra Nevada, and the Columbia Plateau. The largest of these is the Great Basin, an **arid** area in which dozens of north-south mountain ranges alternate with flat valley floors. When the snow on the mountaintops melts, it can create rivers that flow through the valleys. However, the sun often **evaporates** this water as fast as it is supplied. The mountains of the Sierra Nevada are confined mostly to eastern California, but they extend into west-central Nevada as well. The Columbia Plateau, in the northeast, is part of a high prairie that also covers much of Oregon and Idaho. The Mojave Desert, located largely in southeastern California, also covers the southern tip of Nevada.

MOJAVE DESERT

The vast Mojave Desert covers the southern tip of the state and parts of California, Utah, and Arizona.

LAKE TAHOE

Located in the Sierra Nevada range, freshwater Lake Tahoe is a popular destination for tourists.

RED ROCK CANYON

Visitors can hike and picnic at Red Rock Canyon, which is part of the Mojave Desert.

COLORADO RIVER

The Colorado River is the lowest point in the state, at 479 feet above sea level.

Nevada gets its name from its beautiful snowcapped mountains. The Spanish word *nevada* means "snow covered."

The Humboldt River is the longest river in Nevada. It runs for more than 300 miles through the northern part of the state.

Lake Mead is one of the largest human-made lakes in the world. It was created when Hoover Dam was built across the Colorado River.

The red sandstone formations in Valley of Fire National Park were created by shifting sand dunes.

Many parts of Nevada experience scorching summer temperatures.

Climate

T he high mountains of the Sierra Nevada force clouds to drop most of their moisture in California. As a result, very little **precipitation** falls east of the mountains in Nevada. Much of the state is desert, with large areas averaging less than nine inches of precipitation a year. The coolest area is the northeast, where summer temperatures average around 70° Fahrenheit and winters have readings around 25° F. The southern area near Las Vegas, on the other hand, has a winter average of 47° F. Las Vegas summers are very hot, with temperatures often reaching well over 100° F.

Average July Temperatures Across Nevada

Nevada's summer temperatures vary widely across the state. What geographical features might contribute to Las Vegas's July temperatures being so much higher than Carson City's?

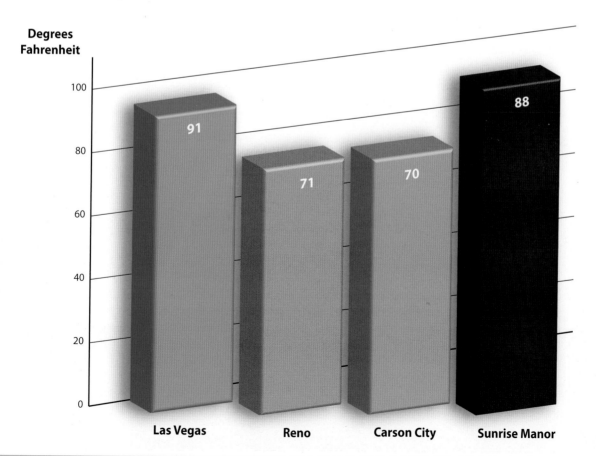

Degrees Fahrenheit

- Las Vegas: 91
- Reno: 71
- Carson City: 70
- Sunrise Manor: 88

There are about 20 active gold mines in Nevada.
After it is mined, gold is melted to remove impurities.

Natural Resources

Nevada's soil is very poor, and water is limited. This makes agriculture less important than it is in most other states. The state's rich natural resources are found deep in the Earth. Nevada is called the Silver State for a very good reason. A lot of silver has been dug from Nevada's hills. But gold is now the most important mineral, with Nevada leading the nation in gold production. Many other minerals are also produced in the state.

Nevada is rich in precious stones. Turquoise, known as the Jewel of the Desert, is found in several deposits in the state. North America's richest vein of black fire opal is also located in Nevada. It is found in the Virgin Valley in the northern part of the state. Black fire opal is Nevada's official precious gemstone.

Nevada is known for its turquoise and silver jewelry.

Plants

Nevada has a fragile environment. With so little moisture in the state, there is a fine line between life and death for plants and animals. Humans have been tough on Nevada's environment, too. After World War II, the federal government tested nuclear bombs less than 100 miles northwest of Las Vegas. Still, from mountain peaks to deserts, Nevada has a wide variety of vegetation. Hearty trees grow in the mountains, and the desert supports many types of cacti.

JOSHUA TREE

Joshua trees, the largest member of the yucca family, are found in the Mojave Desert in the southern part of the state.

BRISTLECONE PINE

Nevada's mountains are home to Bristlecone pines. These trees can live for more than 4,000 years.

SAGEBRUSH

Sagebrush, the low shrub that is Nevada's state flower, grows throughout the state. It has a strong smell that helps discourage animals from eating it.

CALIFORNIA POPPY

The California poppy, often seen along roadsides in Nevada, closes its petals at night or when it is very cold.

More than 30 types of cactus grow in Nevada.

The single-leaf lupine, which grows in rocky soil and often reaches heights of about 15 feet, shares with the bristlecone pine the designation of official state tree of Nevada.

The Ethel M Botanical Cactus Garden in Las Vegas is home to more than 300 types of plants.

In 1999, Nevada experienced terrible wildfires. Fires burned more than 1.6 million acres, dramatically affecting plants and animals in the northern part of the state.

Animals

Poisonous spiders and many types of lizards make their home in Nevada. Larger animals include bighorn sheep, elk, and mule deer. Wild horses and burros are also found in the state. Because their populations can quickly grow out of control, hundreds are gathered each year and offered for adoption by Nevada residents.

Droughts and wildfires regularly destroy large sections of Nevada's forests and grasslands. Increased human use, grazing, and new invading plant species only make these natural cycles more destructive. This threatens the entire **ecosystem**, including the animals that depend upon **vegetation** for food and shelter.

DESERT TORTOISE

The desert tortoise is Nevada's state reptile. Its forelimbs are adapted for digging through desert sand.

GILA MONSTER

The only poisonous lizard native to the United States, the Gila monster can be found in the southern part of the state.

WESTERN DIAMONBACK

There are five different types of rattlesnake found in Nevada. The largest, the western diamondback, can grow to be as much as four feet long.

MOUNTAIN LION

More than 2,000 mountain lions live in Nevada, though the big cats are rarely seen. They are solitary animals who blend in with their surroundings

The cui-ui is an ancient species of fish that was once a main food of the Paiute people. Now it is found only in Nevada's Pyramid Lake and lower Truckee River. The Truckee River is about 120 miles long and empties into Pyramid Lake in the Great Basin.

Berlin-Ichthyosaur State Park was built to protect about 40 skeletons of ancient sea reptiles, some as large as 50 feet long. Adult ichthyosaurs had huge eyes that were protected with a bony ring.

Most desert bighorn sheep stay tucked away in the mountains of southern Nevada. Only occasionally do they visit the scorching valley floors.

The desert tortoise can live up to 100 years.

Tourism

Gambling and wacky weddings are among the reasons why millions of people visit Nevada each year. In 1931 the state made it legal to gamble in public places. At first most gambling took place at expensive resorts near Reno. But starting in the 1940s casinos sprang up by the dozens in Las Vegas, and people from across the United States began crossing the desert to play in them. Nevada law also makes it easy to marry and divorce. Quick, inexpensive, and unusual wedding ceremonies bring happy couples to the state to say "I do." In Las Vegas couples can get married underwater, while bungee jumping, or even at a 24-hour drive-through window. Starting in the 1920s Reno also became known as the divorce capital of the world.

Over the years tourism has only increased, with new resort areas developing near Laughlin and elsewhere in the state. With all the tourists to feed, make beds for, and deal cards to, the service sector of the economy is Nevada's top employer by far.

LAS VEGAS

The city of Las Vegas is Nevada's most popular tourist destination. Approximately 3 million people visit the city every month.

HOOVER DAM

Many people come to view the enormous Hoover Dam on the Arizona-Nevada border. Completed in 1935, the dam is a National Historic Landmark.

VALLEY OF FIRE STATE PARK

Valley of Fire State Park is Nevada's largest and oldest state park. Visitors can hike, camp, and watch for birds and other wildlife.

PYRAMID LAKE

Scenic Pyramid Lake is one of the largest natural lakes in Nevada.

I DIDN'T KNOW THAT!

Las Vegas is among the top tourist destinations in the United States, especially for Americans traveling within the country.

In 1946 the mobster Bugsy Siegel built a huge casino-hotel named the Flamingo in the dusty desert town of Las Vegas. The Flamingo started the city's trend of flashy buildings packed with entertainment to draw in gamblers.

The Reno Rodeo has been attracting fans since 1919.

Many celebrities have gotten married in Las Vegas, including Angelina Jolie and Britney Spears.

Industry

Nevada leads the nation in gold production and is among the top silver producers. Other major mining products include barite, magnesite, mercury, diatomite, and lithium. One of the country's richest mineral regions extends eastward from California across Nevada and into Arizona.

Industries in Nevada
Value of Goods and Services in Millions of Dollars

Service industries are a major part of the state's economy. People in service industries work in schools, hospitals, and government offices, as well as in places visited by tourists. What are some major services performed by government workers?

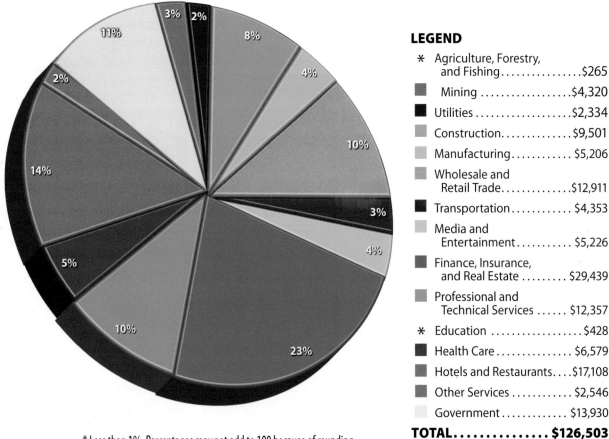

LEGEND

*	Agriculture, Forestry, and Fishing	$265
	Mining	$4,320
	Utilities	$2,334
	Construction	$9,501
	Manufacturing	$5,206
	Wholesale and Retail Trade	$12,911
	Transportation	$4,353
	Media and Entertainment	$5,226
	Finance, Insurance, and Real Estate	$29,439
	Professional and Technical Services	$12,357
*	Education	$428
	Health Care	$6,579
	Hotels and Restaurants	$17,108
	Other Services	$2,546
	Government	$13,930
TOTAL		**$126,503**

* Less than 1%. Percentages may not add to 100 because of rounding.

The dry conditions in Nevada make the state a difficult place for agriculture. However, cattle and sheep are raised in large numbers. Thick grasses in some of the valleys provide good grazing land. Crops such as hay and wheat are also grown to feed these animals. In addition, onions and potatoes are grown in Nevada. Crops are irrigated with river water because of the low rainfall.

Nevada's leading industry is tourism. Millions of tourists travel to the state every year. Casinos, hotels, and restaurants provide jobs for many Nevadans. The state's largest private employer is MGM Resorts, which employs 47,000 people.

Much more of Nevada's agricultural land is used for raising livestock than growing crops.

Gambling is a major industry in the state.

The first federal irrigation project in the state, the Newlands Project, began in 1903. Its dams and canals brought water from near Lake Tahoe to new farmlands in Nevada's western desert.

Nevada is one of seven states with no state income tax. The other states are Alaska, Florida, South Dakota, Texas, Washington, and Wyoming.

Crops grown in Nevada include garlic, potatoes, barley, and mint.

Goods and Services

The majority of Nevadans work in the service sector. A great number of these jobs are in restaurants, hotels, and casinos. The government is also a major employer in the state. The federal government owns more than 80 percent of the land in Nevada, including several large military bases and weapons-testing ranges. Mining and manufacturing also provide jobs for many Nevadans. The state's leading manufactured goods include such food products as processed foods and pet food, plastics, and construction machinery.

The Luxor Hotel in Las Vegas, which is shaped like a pyramid, is one of the largest hotels in the world. It employs many Nevadans.

Water supplies, used for irrigation and electricity generation, are also economically important. In 1933 the first concrete for Hoover Dam was poured. When completed, the 726-foot-high dam backed up the Colorado River for 110 miles in Lake Mead. Water **turbines** in the dam cleanly generate electricity for Arizona, Nevada, and southern California. Lake Mead provides drinking and irrigation water for millions of people in the Southwest and is also popular with boaters and **anglers**.

Lake Mead is more than 100 miles long and up to hundreds of feet deep. The water level in the lake varies depending on the amounts of rainfall and snowfall in mountainous areas farther north.

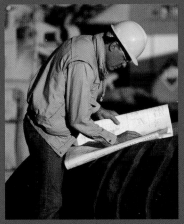

American Indians

Humans hunted mammoths, bison, and reindeer in what is now Nevada many thousands of years ago. Signs of later people have been found painted on rocks and carved in the walls of caves. These wandering hunters left behind stone tools. The first groups to establish settlements in the region were called the Basket Makers. They settled in farming villages and built mud-brick pit houses. They developed large trading networks and irrigation systems for the corn and beans they grew. Later, they learned to make pottery and built their houses above ground. These people, who were probably ancestors of the modern Pueblo Indians, had vanished from Nevada by the 1100s.

Early American Indians of the Nevada region depended on bison and other large animals for food.

The Southern Paiute were hunter-gatherers. They lived in Nevada, Utah, Arizona, and California.

Shoshone, Southern Paiute, Washoe, and Mojave people were all living in Nevada when Europeans arrived in the 1700s. The Shoshone and the Southern Paiute roamed the mountains and valleys in small bands, hunting small game and gathering seeds and plants. They made clothes from rabbit hides and wove baskets for carrying food and possessions. The Washoe fished and hunted deer and antelope near Lake Tahoe and were known for their skill in basketry. The Mojave lived in fertile areas along the Colorado River, growing corn, beans, and squash as well as hunting and fishing. Descendants of all of these people today live on **reservations** and in towns and cities throughout the state.

The Basket Makers used yucca and sagebrush to weave their tightly coiled baskets.

Nevada was grassland, not desert, 10,000 years ago. The early peoples of Nevada had plenty of freshwater in lakes around the state.

Camels were used as pack animals in the Nevada region until 1875, when they were outlawed on state highways. Many escaped or were turned loose in the desert, and as late as the 1930s wild herds of the animals were seen.

Explorers and Missionaries

While traveling from New Mexico to California in about 1776, the Spanish missionary Father Francisco Garcés became the first European known to set foot in what is now Nevada. Southern Nevada later became part of the Old Spanish Trail from Santa Fe, New Mexico, to Los Angeles, California. In about 1829 a Mexican scout named Rafael Rivera discovered **springs** in the arid valley along the trail. He named the spot Las Vegas, which is Spanish for "the meadows."

Jedediah S. Smith, a fur trader, became the first white American to cross the Sierra Nevada and Nevada's central desert, on his way back from California to Utah in 1826. In 1842, Kit Carson and John C. Frémont started exploring the area for the U.S. government. They surveyed and mapped the entire region, which was largely unknown before their arrival. These maps paved the way for future settlers.

Carson City, the Carson River, and Carson Lake, as well as California's Carson Pass, were all named after Kit Carson.

Timeline of Settlement

Early Exploration

1776 Francisco Garcés is the first European to enter what is now Nevada.

1826 Jedediah S. Smith becomes the first United States citizen to cross the Sierra Nevada and Great Basin.

1829 Rafael Rivera, from Mexico, is the first non-Indian to sight the Las Vegas Valley.

U.S. Exploration and Control

1842 Kit Carson and John C. Frémont start exploring and mapping Nevada for the U.S. government.

1844 Paiute Indian Chief Truckee guides a wagon train from Humboldt Sink to the river that is named for him.

1848 Most of the Southwest, including Nevada, is transferred from Mexico to the United States at the end of the Mexican-American War.

Settlement and Silver

1851 Led by John Reese, a group of Mormons from Salt Lake City establishes the trading post Mormon Station.

1852 Benjamin Palmer is the first African American known to settle in Nevada.

1859 A rich deposit of silver, called the Comstock Lode, is discovered.

Statehood

1861 President James Buchanan signs a bill establishing the Nevada Territory.

1864 Nevada becomes the 36th state on October 31.

Early Settlers

I n 1848 the United States defeated Mexico in the Mexican-American War. The treaty that ended the war gave the United States possession of most of the American Southwest, including what is now Nevada. American settlers began to trickle into the state. In 1851 a group of Mormons from Utah started a trading post they called Mormon Station.

Map of Settlements and Resources in Early Nevada

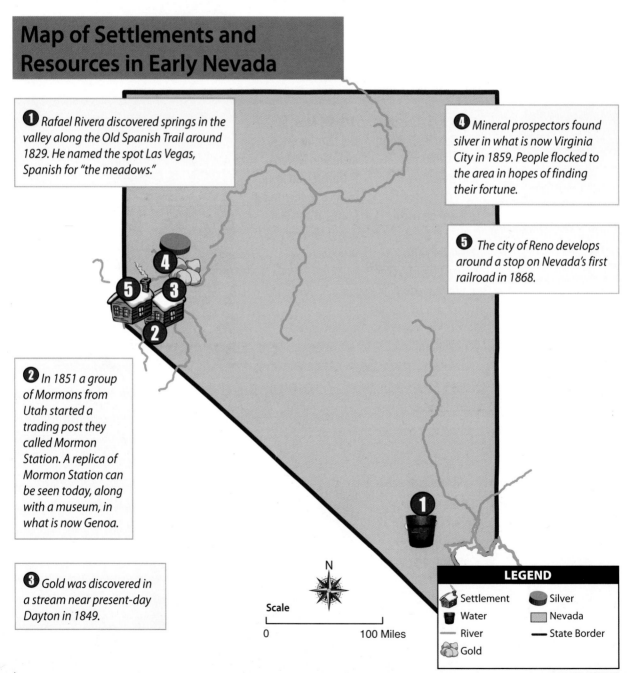

❶ Rafael Rivera discovered springs in the valley along the Old Spanish Trail around 1829. He named the spot Las Vegas, Spanish for "the meadows."

❹ Mineral prospectors found silver in what is now Virginia City in 1859. People flocked to the area in hopes of finding their fortune.

❺ The city of Reno develops around a stop on Nevada's first railroad in 1868.

❷ In 1851 a group of Mormons from Utah started a trading post they called Mormon Station. A replica of Mormon Station can be seen today, along with a museum, in what is now Genoa.

❸ Gold was discovered in a stream near present-day Dayton in 1849.

Scale

0   100 Miles

N

LEGEND

🧰	Settlement	⬮	Silver
🪣	Water	▨	Nevada
—	River	▬	State Border
🪨	Gold		

It was the state's first permanent non-Indian settlement. In 1859 mineral prospectors found silver in Nevada. The Comstock Lode was the nation's largest silver strike up to that point. It brought thousands of prospectors and miners into Nevada. Almost overnight the boomtown of Virginia City appeared near the deposit, bursting at the seams with people coming to make a fortune. It was a lawless town filled with fortune hunters, gamblers, and outlaws.

The U.S. government created the separate Nevada Territory in 1861. Before that, Nevada had been part of the Utah Territory. Nevada's rich silver deposits were important to the Union in the early 1860s, to help pay the costs of the Civil War. In 1864, the year before the Civil War ended, Congress passed and President Abraham Lincoln signed a measure making Nevada a state.

Miners worked in dangerous conditions to extract silver from the Comstock Lode.

The Comstock Lode was named after prospector Henry Comstock, part-owner of the land on which the deposit was found.

In 1849 Mormon settlers established the State of Deseret in what would become Utah and Nevada. Governed by Mormon leader Brigham Young, the area became the Utah Territory in 1850.

During the mineral rush, boomtowns popped up wherever gold and silver were found. Once all the metal had been mined from a site, the town around it simply died as people moved on to the next strike. Since then, **ghost towns** have dotted much of Nevada's landscape.

Miners deep in the Comstock Lode worked in 120° F heat, which was caused by scalding underground water running through the rock beneath them.

Notable People

Many notable Nevadans have contributed to development of their state and country. These people have included a well-known first lady, U.S. Senators and other political leaders, award-winning fashion designers, and business tycoons. Many other major figures have called the great state of Nevada home.

SARAH WINNEMUCCA (1841–1891)

Sarah Winnemucca was the daughter of Northern Paiute Chief Winnemucca. She learned English and became a teacher and translator. She traveled around the world giving lectures, hoping to improve the lives of American Indians. In 1883 she wrote her life story, *Life Among the Paiute*. It was the first book published in English by an American Indian woman.

EDITH HEAD (1897–1981)

Designer Edith Head was born Edith Claire Posener in Searchlight, where her father was an engineer in a gold mine. After moving to California, she was hired by Paramount Pictures to work as a costume sketch artist. She then moved on to costume design, where she created costumes for many famous actors, including Grace Kelly and Natalie Wood. She was nominated for 35 Academy Awards in her career and holds the record for most ever won by a woman, with 8.

PAT NIXON
(1912–1993)

Born Thelma Catherine Ryan in Ely, Pat Nixon attended the University of Southern California and worked as a high school teacher before marrying Richard Nixon in 1940. After her husband was elected president in 1968, she was active in volunteer work and collected hundreds of antiques and pieces of art for the White House collection.

HARRY REID
(1939–)

Harry Reid was born in Searchlight, where his father worked in a gold mine. Reid went to college in Utah and later got a law degree from George Washington University. After working as a lawyer, he was elected to the U.S. House of Representatives in 1982 and the U.S. Senate in 1986. He became the Senate Majority Leader in January 2007.

STEVE WYNN
(1942–)

Steve Wynn, born Stephen Alan Weinberg in Connecticut, is one of the most influential developers in Las Vegas history. He took over his family's bingo business in Maryland in the early 1960s, then moved to Las Vegas and bought part of the Frontier Hotel and Casino in 1967. He later opened many casinos and hotels, including the Bellagio.

I DIDN'T KNOW THAT!

Pat McCarran (1876–1954) was born in Reno. He served as Nevada Chief Justice and chairman of the Nevada State Board of Bar Examiners before becoming a United States Senator. He was a senator for more than 20 years, from 1933 until 1954. McCarran International Airport in Las Vegas is named for him.

Eva Bertrand Adams (1908–1991) was born in Wonder and spent much of her childhood in Reno. After college and graduate school, she worked as an assistant to Senator Pat McCarran. In 1961 President John F. Kennedy asked her to become the director of the U.S. Mint. At the time, it was the highest public position ever held by a woman from Nevada. She was only the second woman to have the job.

Population

Nevada residents have a lot of space in which to live. Nevada is one of the least densely populated states. This means that if you figure out the average amount of the state's area for each member of the population, Nevadans should have a lot of room to themselves. However, large stretches of Nevada have no people at all. More than 90 percent of Nevadans live in the state's few towns, and cities, and suburbs outside the cities.

Nevada Population 1950–2010

In recent decades Nevada's population has grown faster than any other state in the country. What might cause the populations of some states to grow faster than others?

Number of People

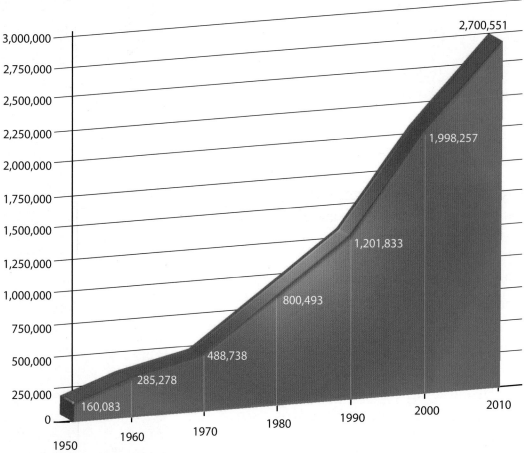

Children make up about one quarter of Nevada's population.

Many of Nevada's early settlers were Mormon. Today, Mormons make up about 7 percent of the state's population.

Before the discovery of the Comstock Lode in 1859, Nevada had only a few thousand settlers.

Nevada's largest county by population is Clark. The county, which includes Las Vegas, is home to about 2 million residents.

In the 1980s Nevada became the fastest-growing state in terms of population. Between 1990 and 2000, Nevada's population increased by 66 percent. From 2000 to 2010, the state's population grew by more than 35 percent, again the highest rate of increase of any state.

The majority of the state's population is of European descent. About 8 percent of Nevadans are African American, and almost 7 percent are of Asian heritage. Native Americans now make up a little less than 2 percent of the population. The largest minority group in Nevada is Hispanic Americans, who may be of any race. More than 26 percent of Nevadans claim Hispanic ancestry.

The State Capitol Building in Carson City was completed in 1871.

Politics and Government

Nevada still operates under the constitution it adopted when it became a state in 1864, although the document has been amended several times. Nevada has often been a step ahead of other states on political issues. In 1905 Nevada began using **referenda** to let voters decide whether to pass certain laws. In 1914, when few places allowed women's **suffrage**, Nevada became one of the first states to give women the right to vote in elections.

As in other states, the government of Nevada consists of three branches. They are the executive, the legislative, and the judicial. The governor and other officials of the executive branch are elected for four-year terms. The legislative branch is made up of a 21-member Senate, with four-year terms, and a 42-member Assembly, whose members are elected every two years. The Supreme Court is the highest court in the judicial branch. Nevada is divided into 16 counties, plus the independent capital of Carson City.

Brian Sandoval was elected governor of Nevada in November 2010. He became the state's first Hispanic American governor.

Cultural Groups

The majority of Nevadans have European ancestry. Most trace their roots back to Germany, Great Britain, Spain, or Ireland. One distinct European group in Nevada is the Basques. Their sheep-herding ancestors came from the Pyrenees Mountains in Spain and France. Basque people from across the country come to the National Basque Festival at Elko every July. Handball, bread baking, and wood chopping are among the traditional competitions held at the festival. In the wood chopping contest, each contestant must chop through seven logs.

"Cowboy culture" is widely celebrated in Nevada. The Reno Rodeo is one of the most popular rodeos in the country.

Hispanic culture is an important part of Nevada's heritage. The Latin Grammy Awards, which celebrate Spanish and Portuguese music, were held in Las Vegas in 2010.

There are several American Indian reservations in Nevada. People living on these reservations attempt to keep their traditions alive in a quickly changing world. Off the reservations, American Indians gather and celebrate their traditions at powwows and festivals. Nevada also has an active cowboy culture. Through events such as the Reno Rodeo, Frontier Days, and Nevada Day, Nevadans honor their cowboy and pioneer traditions.

The Lost City Museum in Overton displays a Pueblo Indian archaeological site as well as artifacts from around the region. Some of the items are 10,000 years old.

The Mexican holiday Cinco de Mayo is celebrated with a festival in Reno every year. The festival features traditional Mexican crafts, food, and music. Proceeds from the event are donated to a nonprofit group called Nevada Hispanic Services.

Humboldt Museum in Winnemucca exhibits American Indian and pioneer artifacts.

Most of Nevada's American Indians are Paiute. One of the most famous Paiute in history was Wovoka, a religious leader.

Arts and Entertainment

Though Las Vegas was born as a remote getaway for gamblers, over the years it has added entertainment options for many other tastes as well. Several casinos have built attractions especially for families. The Excalibur Hotel is shaped like a medieval castle. The hotel showcases magicians, jugglers, and puppeteers. At the Mirage, smoke and flames erupt out of an **artificial** volcano surrounded by a lagoon and dozens of waterfalls. Inside the hotel are a miniature rain forest, live white tigers, and a family of bottlenose dolphins living in a giant saltwater pool. The Circus Circus Adventuredome is an indoor amusement park that offers roller coasters and water slides.

There are nearly 4,000 rooms in the Excalibur Hotel in Las Vegas.

Many movies have featured scenes filmed inside the Circus Circus, including *Baby Geniuses* and *Honey, I Blew Up the Kid.*

Actress Rutina Wesley was born in Las Vegas. Her father, Ivery Wheeler, is a professional tap dancer.

The Lied Discovery Children's Museum in Las Vegas features a model tornado.

At the time it was built, the Mirage was the most expensive hotel-casino in history.

Las Vegas is famous for its live entertainment offerings. Famous jazz, country-western, rock, and pop singers from across the country perform in Vegas lounges every night. Comedians and dancers also entertain on the city's many stages.

Museums in Nevada range from monuments to the building of Hoover Dam to a three-dimensional look at *Guinness World Records.* More traditional museums display fossils or artifacts of the region's early American Indian cultures.

For a different look at Nevada's past, people can visit one of the state's many ghost towns. Old-fashioned cattle drives can also be arranged. Riding a horse across the desert will calm anyone after the chaos of Nevada's glamorous side.

Sports

Nevada offers a wide variety of traditional and newly emerging sports for all seasons. Skiing, snowboarding, and snowshoeing are popular in the mountains. Fly-fishing in Nevada's rivers, streams, and lakes is a favorite way to spend summer days. A new sport gaining popularity in Nevada is disc golf. Played on courses in parks and forests, the sport is like golf but uses a flying disc rather than a ball. Metal baskets are designated as the "holes" that players are to hit with the disc. Most golfers in Nevada play the traditional version of the game, which is possible nearly year-round thanks to the region's warm climate.

Nevada is also host to several major sporting events. The National Finals Rodeo is held in Las Vegas. It is the biggest rodeo in the country, and the prize money draws riders and wranglers from across the United States. There are no professional sports teams in the state, but the University of Las Vegas, or UNLV, has one of the most successful basketball programs in the country.

Nevada is home to more than 15 ski resorts.

Freestyle skier Shannon Bahrke was born in Reno. She won a bronze medal at the 2010 Winter Olympics.

The UNLV basketball team, the Runnin' Rebels, draws huge crowds at the Thomas & Mack Center in Las Vegas.

I DIDN'T KNOW THAT!

Born in Las Vegas, Andre Agassi was the youngest American tennis player ever to be ranked the best in the world. In 1999 he became only the fifth man in history to win all four Grand Slam tennis tournaments. Several of those tournaments he won twice or more.

Although golf is usually played on lush green grass, some courses in Nevada have adapted the sport to the arid climate. On those courses golf is played on clay and sand.

Virginia City hosts the International Camel Races each year in honor of the days when camels were used to pack supplies around the Comstock Lode.

Nevada's first skiers were miners who used skis to quickly get from place to place in the heavy snows of the Sierra Nevada.

National Averages Comparison

The United States is a federal republic, consisting of fifty states and the District of Columbia. Alaska and Hawai'i are the only non-contiguous, or non-touching, states in the nation. Today, the United States of America is the third-largest country in the world in population. The United States Census Bureau takes a census, or count of all the people, every ten years. It also regularly collects other kinds of data about the population and the economy. How does Nevada compare to the national average?

Comparison Chart

Statistic	USA	Nevada
Admission to Union	NA	October 31, 1864
Land Area (in square miles)	3,537,438.44	109,825.99
Population Total	308,745,538	2,700,551
Population Density (people per square mile)	87.28	24.59
Population Percentage Change (April 1, 2000, to April 1, 2010)	9.7%	35.1%
White Persons (percent)	72.4%	66.2%
Black Persons (percent)	12.6%	8.1%
American Indian and Alaska Native Persons (percent)	0.9%	1.2%
Asian Persons (percent)	4.8%	7.2%
Native Hawaiian and Other Pacific Islander Persons (percent)	0.2%	0.6%
Some Other Race (percent)	6.2%	12.0%
Persons Reporting Two or More Races (percent)	2.9%	4.7%
Persons of Hispanic or Latino Origin (percent)	16.3%	26.5%
Not of Hispanic or Latino Origin (percent)	83.7%	73.5%
Median Household Income	$52,029	$56,432
Percentage of People Age 25 or Over Who Have Graduated from High School	80.4%	80.7%

*All figures are based on the 2010 United States Census, with the exception of the last two items.

How to Improve My Community

Strong communities make strong states. Think about what features are important in your community. What do you value? Education? Health? Forests? Safety? Beautiful spaces? Government works to help citizens create ideal living conditions that are fair to all by providing services in communities. Consider what changes you could make in your community. How would they improve your state as a whole? Using this concept web as a guide, write a report that outlines the features you think are most important in your community and what improvements could be made. A strong state needs strong communities.

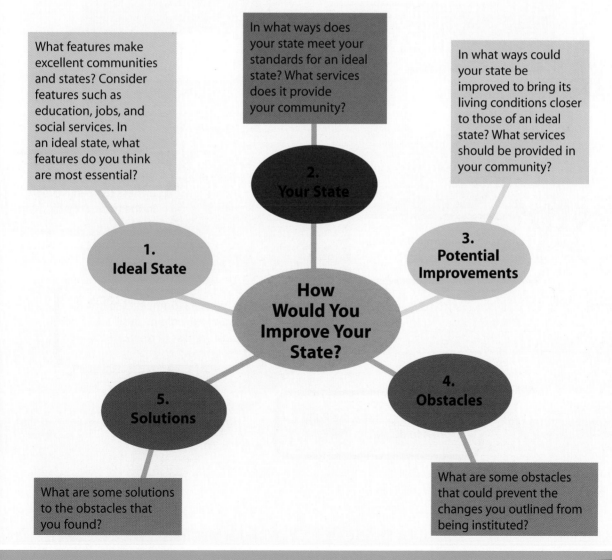

What features make excellent communities and states? Consider features such as education, jobs, and social services. In an ideal state, what features do you think are most essential?

In what ways does your state meet your standards for an ideal state? What services does it provide your community?

In what ways could your state be improved to bring its living conditions closer to those of an ideal state? What services should be provided in your community?

2.
Your State

1.
Ideal State

3.
Potential
Improvements

How
Would You
Improve Your
State?

4.
Obstacles

5.
Solutions

What are some solutions to the obstacles that you found?

What are some obstacles that could prevent the changes you outlined from being instituted?

Exercise Your Mind!

Think about these questions and then use your research skills to find the answers and learn more fascinating facts about Nevada. A teacher, librarian, or parent may be able to help you locate the best sources to use in your research.

1 Are there alien life forms in Nevada?

2 Where is the Loneliest Road in America?

3 Why is the California National Historic Trail in Nevada?

4 Did Nevada ever use the Pony Express to deliver its mail?

5 What popular article of clothing was invented by Jacob Davis, a tailor from Reno?

6 What is a "rising room"?

7 What was the most lawless town in Nevada in the mid-1800s?

8 Who was Samuel Clemens and how did he raise awareness of Nevada?

Words to Know

anglers: people who fish

arid: very dry

artificial: not occurring naturally

barren: lacking plant life

burros: small donkeys

casinos: places where people go to gamble

ecosystem: a natural environment, the living things within it, and the relationship between them

evaporates: changes from liquid to gas

ghost towns: towns that have been deserted

impersonators: people who mimic the voice, appearance, and mannerisms of other people

irrigate: to water land through artificial methods

precipitation: moisture that falls to Earth in the form of rain or snow

referenda: ballots allowing citizens to vote on laws

replica: a copy or imitation

reservations: lands set aside for American Indians to live on

springs: openings at or near the surface of the Earth through which water from underground sources emerges

suffrage: the right to vote

turbines: devices that create electricity from the flow of water, steam, or gas

vegetation: plant life

Index

Log on to www.av2books.com

AV² by Weigl brings you media enhanced books that support active learning. Go to www.av2books.com, and enter the special code found on page 2 of this book. You will gain access to enriched and enhanced content that supplements and complements this book. Content includes video, audio, web links, quizzes, a slide show, and activities.

Audio
Listen to sections of the book read aloud.

Video
Watch informative video clips.

Embedded Weblinks
Gain additional information for research.

Try This!
Complete activities and hands-on experiments.

WHAT'S ONLINE?

Try This!	Embedded Weblinks	Video	EXTRA FEATURES
Test your knowledge of the state in a mapping activity.	Discover more attractions in Nevada.	Watch a video introduction to Nevada.	**Audio** Listen to sections of the book read aloud.
Find out more about precipitation in your city.	Learn more about the history of the state.	Watch a video about the features of the state.	
Plan what attractions you would like to visit in the state.	Learn the full lyrics of the state song.		**Key Words** Study vocabulary, and complete a matching word activity.
Learn more about the early natural resources of the state.			
Write a biography about a notable resident of Nevada.			**Slide Show** View images and captions, and prepare a presentation.
Complete an educational census activity.			**Quizzes** Test your knowledge.

AV² was built to bridge the gap between print and digital. We encourage you to tell us what you like and what you want to see in the future.
Sign up to be an AV² Ambassador at www.av2books.com/ambassador.